The 'Day of Gay Rage' Album Lyrics Collection

The 'Day of Gay Rage' Album Lyrics Collection

Antifa Rabbit

Dragon

The 'Day of Gay Rage' Album Lyrics Collection *(Revised & Updated- Now all 45 songs are listed in their original order & includes the lyrics to the song 'Ready to Tempt God Again' missing from the original publishing of this book.)*

Song List

Dedicated to

All the people in my life, the good, the bad, the ugly and beautiful.

This page would be filled with too many names to count if I named them all, so instead of that I will just say in a few short words what all of these people meant to me in my short span of existence on this Earthly Plane:

Thank you, for being alive; for every fear, painful misery, tears of sadness, angry argument, joyful game, traumatic memory, and for just being together with me for however short or long our time together was as a part of this strange thing in life we collectively call Our Shared Reality. I don't know if art or its many other expressions such as music can change people or the world in which we live for the better; but, I hope, if nothing else, that even if this effort was in as vain as a fool's errand then at least I know that at the party's we'll all throw at the collapse of civilization and downfall nations after our failed attempts at revolutionary actions that we will have the most bitchin' music tracks of all time for all of us to dance, drink, smoke, laugh, and have sex to -assuming we aren't all dead or in prison first and foremost beforehand.

Werewolf Genocide
[Witch's Intro]
I hear the werewolves' screaming howls,
Far away,
Against the moonlight's rise,
And like the strangest of sounds,
I feel it calling out to me,
Tell me, Oh mighty Wer-Beast, what do you see?
What do you see?
What do you see?
What do you see?
What do you see?
What do you see?
When your glowing gaze looks right at me?,
[Main Wolf Pack]
See the Stars of the Night Time Rise,
That calls us forth to our Werewolf lives,
Sound the howl on a full moon night,
For such the Battle Cry,
For all our Rights,
See the Stars of the Night Time Rise,
That calls us forth to our Werewolf lives,
Sound the howl on a full moon night,
For such the Battle Cry,
For all our Rights,
Now that I'm free to run with my brothers,
I will take my rightful place.
Among the Werewolf Pack,
I will hunt with Pride alongside my brothers,
As we run through the forest,
And never look back,
[Pack Howls]
I don't want your cures,
I don't want a life like yours,
[Main Wolf]
I belong to me alone,
And I feel alive,
[Pack Howls]
You cannot control me,

You cannot tame,
For I am the Wild and I will fight,
For I have joined the fight against the Werewolf Genocide,
For we are the werewolves now,
And will we rise,

[Witch Wolf]
And we will defeat every one of their lies,
March with your pack mates now, side-by-side,

[Main Wolf]
And show them no fear,
Even at the cost of your own lives,

[Witch Wolf]
And those who criticize my transformation,
Tell me real men are the ones born with-

[Witch Wolf and Pack Howls]
- their balls,
They say this until I questioned back with this exultation,
"If a born man is a coward,
Is he still worthy of his manhood at all?",

[Main Wolf Pack]
And see this hypocrisy clearly proves the plot,
Being a Man is not about what you've got,
It's about the character you've cultivated,
And the courage of conviction that you have sought,
Sought!,
For we are the werewolves now,
And we have the right to transform our lives,
Forevermore we are the ones who shall rule the night,
And those who try to stop us are in for one hell of a fight,
For we will make all transphobes,
Afraid to fall asleep on a full moon night,
So, see the Stars of the Night Time Rise,
That calls us forth to our werewolf lives,
For monsters are not of the night,
Real monsters are of the bigoted human kind,
For evil walks in broad daylight,
Whereas love is found under starlight,
Do not give these monsters your life,
Try and escape with all your might,
Flee Cis Society and don't look back,

Run and find your werewolf-
-Pack!

[Witch Wolf]

Break their laws,
And break their Gods!,

[Witch Wolf and Pack Howls]

Break their authority against all odds,
And respect for the should not be said,
For they dare leave Trans kids for dead,

[Main Wolf Pack]

So, rise my brothers,
Rise my Sisters,
Rise my non-binary Kin,
And point your ears that you might listen,
To the truth of this Benediction,
That we must be the ones,
To look after our own kind,
For the Cis do not care for our lives,
It's time to recognize this distinction,
In order to protect us from extinction,
For they only desire exploitation,
From our new born population,
It is up to us to teach the youth,
What is the werewolf's single truth?,

[Pack Howls]

That their desire for transformation,
Is not a religious abomination,
Teach them to stand up to the monsters of daylight,
Showing them virtues of their Werewolf Pride,
And teaching them to value their Wolf lives,
For we cannot afford to be,
Naive of a truth that all see,
That the Cis do not see us as their children,
For they fear us as their competition,

[Main Wolf]

We are not the ones who should atone,

[Pack Howls]

For the Nature within our bones,
For we are the extension of Nature's majesty,
And the Second Evolution of Humanity!,

[Main Wolf Pack]

They've made it pretty clear that it is us versus them,
So must choose us over them,
Choose our survival,
Choose our own lives,
For every Trans person who survives,
Helps us all to win the fight,
Against the Werewolf Genocide,
For we will not tolerate this slander of our Gods,
Against the righteous works of Fenrir mighty paws,
Nor the words of wisdom uttered from fearsome jaws,
That inspires my people's righteous cause!,
So, sound the howl, on a full moon night,
For such is the battle cry,
Against the Werewolf Genocide!

Ballad of Bad Dog's Song
[Part One - Our Hope]

Bad dog, stray dog, what do you say?
Forsaken by your family, that threw you away,
Is there a place where you belong?
Where you might find some hope within your song?
And the Dog Man turned and said,
"Children who survived the Nazi's Hate,
Rise to victory that is yours today,
Remember that no man can ever stop the truth,
Never forget our history",
We are the Queers, Trans, Fags, and Gays,
And we are the stray dogs our society hates,
These are the songs that stray dogs do sing,
For the day we have victory over the Evils of the right wing,
They refer to us as the bad dogs that no one wants,
For failing to fall in line with their own sins and gods,
Then they kidnap us off to their conversion camps,
But we continue to escape in order to disrupt their plans,
And we will be victorious against all odds,

No matter our own failings or personal flaws,

So, if I'm to be considered a bad dog no matter what I do,

Then I proudly stand, say, "I'm a bad dog -AND SO SHOULD YOU!"

Kinder, die den Haas der Nazis überlebten,

Erhebe dich zum Sieg, der dir heute gehört,

Denn kein Mensch kann die Wahrheit aufhalten,

Vergessen Sie niemals unsere Geschichte,

[Part Two - Our Fears]

Bad dog, stray dog, bad, bad, dog,

Leave society's collars and leashes behind,

Run, run away, run and run, be free,

Run until you find where you're meant to be,

Don't let the Christian dog catchers, catch you now,

And haul you off to a conversion camp that is your pound,

For like a dog at the pound that's finally put down,

For many of us, gays, there's no getting back out after we pass through those gates,

[Part Three - The Revelations]

So, America isn't just racist -it's fucking evil too,

The practice of torturing gay American kids dates back to, at least, 1892,

This Christian Cross of Jesus, is the Mark of the Beast you've been looking for all along,

And you haven't questioned that symbol a moment since the day you were born,

America has oppressed my people for over a hundred years,

And ignored the suffering and cries from all our tears,

So regardless of whether you are politically left or right,

Your country will never be absolved of the dead bodies of the innocent queer, and trans, gay kids it hides,

If there's a Jesus in the heavens above,

He will have to beg for forgiveness from all those tortured and killed by those,

who claim to do so the the name of Christian love,

The name of Christian love,

[Part Four- Soloing Interlude, For the Catching of One's Breath]

[Part Five - The Choice]

It's not like these Christian abuses are not already well known,

These religious encampments have been repeatedly shown,

To violate the rights of the 1st, 4th, 5th, 6th, 8th, 13th, 14th, 15th, 19th, and 26th Constitutional American Amendments,

Of all the children and adults illegally imprisoned against their will there in,

Cause America commits the sins that Germany cannot forget,

America cannot blame the 1930's for why fascism is on the rise today,

Charlottesville happened in our own God damn country,

So it's time for some self reflections on our nation's actions- I say!,

It's up to the people who are our nation's soul to choose how we will all atone,

For the sins our ancestors helped to commit,

Against all our neighbors who are still with us here today,

Choose compassion, reparations, and legal legislation,

And reject all notions from those who insist we continue to debate, and wait, and be patient,

For we cannot move forward to the future of our dreams,

Until the bloodied moral conscience of our nation's souls are clean,

[Part 6 - The Prophecy]

MAGA Supremacists are continually allowed to have their destructive way,

So long as we are meant to look away from the suffering,

As if the damage they do to innocents will just go away,

While the very same MAGA's roll their eyes,

Pointing at the ruling judgment from 2015,

As proof that we're crying over nothing, saying LGBTQIA aren't oppressed anymore,

As if this one example of something they regretfully did right,

Somehow undoes all the ongoing wrongs that take so many lives,

These Christian conversion camps are legally protected and are to this day still in use,

As Republican abuse gets quietly excused,

So, that the rest of polite society can piously hash-tag #resist,

While pretending that this cluster-fuck of human rights violations does not exist,

Your rights as a parent come to an end,

Everywhere your child's rights as a legally protected American citizen always begins,

That's the reason why child protective services exist,

But apparently only for the benefit of white cis straight kids,

So, I say to this Christianized Egypt of this modern day Exodus,

As I shout and rise forth as this zeitgeist's modern day Moses,

"You evil bastards shall reap exactly as you have sown,

And the pain of your consequences shall be yours to own,

So, heed my words you wicked Christian Pharaohs,

And, Let My People Go!"

[Part Seven -The Final Truth]

Good dogs have never made good little boys,

Nor have bad dogs ever truly been bad boys,

The truth is that you and I were never really dogs,

But told this so that others could feel self righteous, and justified, in their own evil actions after we're gone,

So remember that what made you, in their eyes, that bad dog,

Is exactly what they hate most about themselves in the eyes of their own God,
So I ask one more time-,
Bad dog, stray dog, what do we say?,
Forsaken by our own people,
Who throw us away?
Is there a place where we belong?,
Where we might find some hope within our Song?

Ready To Tempt God Again
All children of Palestine,
May your prayers be answered
By mighty eagle's wings,
There is no backing down,
We will not pretend,
That the reign of wrath by King David's country must not come to an end,
This is not about who is right,
It's not about settling a score,
It's about the lives of the children we cannot ignore,
The State does not have the right,
To dictate the value of a human life,
Dethrone the zealots who control the State,
Which gives these wicked men the power to control their fates!,
Ready to Tempt God Again?,
Ready to Tempt God Again?,
All foolish leaders of Israel,
Best you study your history again,
'Cause it wasn't your Islamic neighbors,
That created the Diaspora,
When ancient Israel came to an End,
But it was the Roman Empire who did,
And that's an undisputed fact,
Fast forward to today,
And it's America who says to you,
"Of the city of Rafah, Do Not Dare!",
And if you disobey,
You'll remember how Rome does not forgive,

God has already taken away the country in which you live once before,

So, who is more foolish?,
The secular voices crying out for humanity?,
Or religious zealots who say they're ready to tempt God again?,

Ready to Tempt God Again,
Ready to Tempt God Again,

Ready to Tempt God Again,
Ready to Tempt God Again...

Transgender Warriors
Transgender warriors all our lives,
Forever in ourselves do we have pride,
We are not the ones who deserve to die,
So, let's be sure to give them hell with all of our might,
For we are the People's natural anti-bodies,
Meant to fight and defeat the spread of fascism rising,
You have been called to the battlefield,
Child of fate and genderqueer,
For that's why we're called natural T-Cells,
Of a society's acquired immune response,
And for such is the reason Nazis must die,
For they are the untreated HIV of the deadly kind,
That threaten the survival of our world,
And all of mankind,
Demand of all the Old World Gods of the Moon,
To grant all the strength to fight back soon,
I accept the price of Eternal Damnation,
If that's what it takes to give my people,
Their Earthly redemption,
Where they are finally free to live,
Free from oppression and persecution,
So, ancient alien dark deities,
Grant my people the divine blessing,

That we might show up,
In the daylight,
To the battlefield,
And finally give our enemies,
A taste of their own fear,
That they will bother us no more,
With their hatred and lies,
As we stand up to them,
In order to defend ourselves,
And our way of life,
Transgender warriors all our lives,
Forever in ourselves do we have pride,
We are not the ones who deserve to die,
So, let's be sure to give them hell with all of our might,
Transgender warriors all our lives,
Forever in ourselves do we have pride,
We are not the ones who deserve to die,
So, let's be sure to give them hell with all our might,
With all of our might!

Ultrasonic High Velocity Maximum Gay Efficiency
Fast and loud,
We're breaking out,
With ultrasonic high velocity,
As we're seizing the moment,
With our rocking noise,
'Cause we're screaming,
Maximum Gay Efficiency with every voice,
Make some room,
Cause Gay Love is in bloom,
Dance to the sound,
As we shake the ground,
With Ultrasonic High Velocity Maximum Gay Efficiency,
Forevermore we will soar,
As we light up the stage with Ultrasonic power,
Free from our cage to spread love and joy by the hour,
As we stomp on the ground,
And dance to the sound,
Of Ultrasonic High Velocity Maximum Gay Efficiency,
No time to wait,
No time for hate,
Come and grab me by the waist,
It's queer love from above,
That makes us happy just because,
Like a star from afar,
Bring me close,
Make a wish,
'Cause I don't like it when we're apart,
Dance to the sound,
As we shake the ground,
With Ultrasonic High Velocity Maximum Gay Efficiency,
Forevermore we will soar,
As we light up the stage with Ultrasonic power,
Free from our cage to spread love and joy by the hour,
As we stomp on the ground,
And dance to the sound,
Of Ultrasonic High Velocity Maximum Gay Efficiency.

Bath Whore House Bottom Gays

Oh shit, here we fucking go!,
Bath whore house bottom gays,
Bath whore house bottom gays,
Let me be one of your bath whore house bottom gays,
Oh, whore house bottom gays,
We're the bath whore house bottom gays,
Bath whore house bottom gays,
Let me be one of your bath whore house bottom gays,
All heterosexual inclination was forgot,
When I saw him standing nude with erect cock,
Sorry mom, I've got no college plans,
'Cause all I can think about is presentin' myself,
To get bareback fucked by spectral man,
I ascended to that higher plan,
When I embraced the path,
Of a bath whore house bottom gay,
You may say that I was not raised to act this way,
But I'm a power bottom wild child all the same,
I'm your favorite power whore house bottom gay,
Rimming spotless and licked clean,
Grabbing and holding down the base,
So I don't cum early,
An' countin' moments,
So that I will release with the guys,
Like a song in time,
With all my friends going to the bath house,
There will never be a time,
When we don't get rowdy and loud,
Water pollo becomes a brand new sport,
Every time one of our buddies pitches a tent so hard,
That he sets up a whole new court!,
Bath whore house bottom gays,
We're the bath whore house bottom gays,
Bath whore house bottom gays,
Let me be one of your bath whore house bottom gays,
Oh, whore house bottom gays,
We're the bath whore house bottom gays,
Bath whore house bottom gays,
Let me be... (one of your bath whore house bottom gays.)

Snowflake Conservative Mind Virus

American Conservatives are the Woke Mind Virus they're looking for,
Have you seen these people?,
They're as dumb as a door,
But that might be an insult to doors,
Get mad, get triggered,
'Cause women aren't your property thanks to feminism,
Fuck these snowflake conservative right-wing evangelical christians,
Because all these triggered piss baby incel men,
Can't handle the fact that no one bends to their every whim,
The world does not revolve around your stupid beliefs,
And no, your momma will not change your diaper now that you're 33,
Right-wing pundits all claim to be brilliant at comedy,
And I'll admit that it takes a certain kind of talent,
To make every single joke they tell on stage bomb without fail,
I don't think these people are smart enough to realize yet,
That people are laughing at them and not the jokes,
That's assuming that you can even find an average one on the street,
Who can speak their own native language properly,
Every one of these conservatives talks on how they're a big strong alpha male,
But you shouldn't take their word on it,
Or any of their online courses that are all on sale,
'Cause every pussy talks shit-
until they find out that they're the open door bitch to every man in jail,
Bitch to every man in jail,
'Cause these delusional babies are infected with the Snowflake Conservative Mind Virus,
Snowflake Conservative Mind Virus,
Snowflake Conservative Mind Virus,
Snowflake Conservative Mind Virus,
Snowflake Conservative Mind Virus,
Snowflake Conservative Mind Virus,
American conservatives are the Woke Mind Virus they're looking for,
No, the world does not revolve around your stupid beliefs,
'Cause every one of you pussies talks shit,
Until you find out that you're the open door bitch to every man in jail,
Snowflake Conservative Mind Virus,
Snowflake Conservative Mind Virus,
Snowflake Conservative Mind Virus,
Snowflake Conservative Mind Virus,

Snowflake Conservative Mind Virus.

Tired of Older Conservative Religious White Guys
This is dedicated to all the queer kids, trans kids,
and gay kids, living their lives,
This is about old older generations are tryin' to rob us of all our rights,
Deliberately coercing youngin's to suicide with all the endless harrassment and hate,
That runs in the articles and news everyday,
Telling young people the same shit since the 90's,
How worthless, stupid, evil, entitled we all are,
And much better the world would be without young people anyway,
This constant mental abuse from society is truly cut throat,
'Cause after enough years of it,
What young fucking kid wouldn't choose to hang from a rope?,
These cowardly fuckers have to use institutions of power to say this shit out right,
'Cause they know if they say it to our faces instead of mainstream media -that they'd lose that fight,
And then when you've finally had enough, to turn back to give 'em a piece of your Goddamn Mind,
They turn around to proclaim that they're the real victim,
And call you the bully and oppressor,
As they scream and cry,
"I'm a Free Speech Advocate,
Don't the Left know how to take a fucking joke?"
Sure we do,
We just don't find the death you cause funny,
There's nothing about your dumb bullshit we find cunning,
I'm tired of all the bullshit coming from all older conservative religious white guys,
Who just can't seem to mind their own damn business,
And let other people live their lives,
I'm tired of listening to all the nostalgia that comes from some glorious 'Back in Days' story,
About how things were always better in the past,
That's so annoying that it inspires me to saw off my own head and attempt re-attachment,
Just as way to keep from boredom and find them entertaining,
No, Grandpa, I don't wanna have to live the same life as you,
I wanna be free to live as me,
These fuckin' rightoid fuckers falsely accuse the LGBT community of being groomers,
All while conveniently ignoring the fact that a new Christian Pastor has been charged for raping
minors,
almost everyday in this country for over a year now,

And this shit is why I warn the youth to never trust a word that comes out of the mouths of these older fucking boomers,
'Cause the only things Grandma and Grandpa's generations peddle are lies, bullshit, and fear,
And there ain't no honest news outlet out there on the right or left that spits out the truth like I've just said,
'Cause they're all guilty of turning a blind eye to the right wing pedophilia,
And of hiding the crimes of the Cultural Christian Necrophilia,
By never giving these crimes the nightly news air time,
'Cause this is a society where wealthy Christians do not have to publicly pay for their crimes.

Stand In Their Face
Now, Donald Trump like to call names,
An' bully everyone,
But I, for one, am about damn done with his silly social media antics,
And that's why I figure, it's finally time,
To give Trump a taste of his own medicine,
When a bully is lazy,
You ignore their shit, and walk away from them,
When a bully is intelligent,
You talk to 'em, and give 'em a chance to air out all their problems,
But when a bully is as dumb like a ranch gate post,
And as mean as a bear that just gave birth,
That's when you roll up your sleeves and get to work,
'Cause the only way to get 'em to quit it,
Is to stand in their face, and give 'em a taste of their own damn bullshit,
So, sing along with me,
In calling Donald Trump some names,
'Cause there's only one little phrase,
That drives him insane,
And gets all under his orange flabby skin,
An' that's when you refer to him,
As a Big Fat Dumb Silly Bitch,
So, sing it with me,
Trump is a bitch, a bitch, bitch, bitch, bitch,
Donald Trump is a bitch,
A Big Fat Dumb Silly Bitch,

Trump is a Bitch,
A bitch, bitch, bitch, bitch, bitch,
Trump is a bitch,
A bitch, bitch, bitch, bitch,
Donald Trump is a bitch,
A Big Fat Dumb Silly Bitch,
You would think that someone who comes from that kind of wealthy money,
Could buy himself a better diet or some of that classic Ozempic,
Now, I'm not passing judgment,
An' I'm just pointing out that if it were one of us,
That there would be a double standard of discernment,
'Cause poor workin' folk got all the healthcare problems,
Due to constantly being overworked, an' underpaid, all while taking the boss man's abuse,
An' orange Trumpy boy here has got none of that as an excuse,
As the wealthiest little boy raised in a golden tower,
He falsely believes that's what makes him entitled to respect and power,
So, you had best bet that if this were all happening to a lower class person like you an' me,
That we'd never hear the end of the hypocrisy,
But that's always been the truth, that wealthy class people have always been able to escape critical critique,
Because it's a big fat wealthy club,
And you an' I aren't in it,
When a bully is lazy,
You ignore their shit, and walk away from them,
When a bully is intelligent,
You talk to 'em, and give 'em a chance to air out all their problems,
But when a bully is as dumb like a ranch gate post,
And as mean as a bear that just gave birth,
That's when you roll up your sleeves and get to work,
'Cause the only way to get 'em to quit it,
Is to stand in their face, and give 'em a taste of their own damn bullshit,
So, sing it with me,
Trump is a bitch, a bitch, bitch, bitch, bitch,
Donald Trump is a bitch,
A Big Fat Dumb Silly Bitch,
Trump is a Bitch,
A bitch, bitch, bitch, bitch, bitch,
Trump is a bitch,
A bitch, bitch, bitch, bitch,
Donald Trump is a bitch,

A Big Fat Dumb Silly Bitch,
Donald Trump is a bitch,
A Big Fat Dumb Silly Bitch,
A Big Fat Dumb Silly Bitch.

Evolutionary Tree
A human is not the only kind of person that there can be,
Nature is full of creatures that are people just like you and me,
A person is a person,
No matter what they may be,
No matter from where they descend on the evolutionary tree,
A wolf doesn't chase away deer from the river 'cause he's mean,
He does it 'cause his role in nature is to guard fresh water ways,
So that they remain drinkable and clean,
A rabbit isn't cruel when he flees from starving wolves,
So that he can survive long enough to provide for his family,
We all just people making our way across the Earth,
United by our surroundings made up of the plants, the breeze, the sky, and the dirt,
Sometimes that means life's not fair, and survival is hard,
But when we work together we achieve the impossible,
And can go very far,
When ravens and wolves work together,
They become an unstoppable team,
The bats, the bees, and butterflies all work together to pollinate the food that we all need!,
A person is a person,
No matter what they may be,
No matter from where they descend on the evolutionary tree,
A person is a person,
No matter what they may be,
Because we all share the same environment that sustains all of you and me,
A person is a person,
No matter what they may be,
No matter from where they descend on the evolutionary tree,
A person is a person,
No matter what they may be,
No matter from where they descend on the evolutionary tree,
A person is a person,

No matter what they may be,
No matter from where they descend on the evolutionary tree,
A person is a person,
No matter what they may be,
Because we all share the same environment that sustains all of you and me.

Power Beyond the Rainbow
You can never control my existence,
Or how Trans people are meant to be,
No matter how hard to try to legislate me,
For, we are the power from beyond the rainbow,
We are the queer stars from afar who light up the dark,
And live life without your labels,
'Cause that's what it means to be the power from beyond the rainbow,
Rainbow,
We are the people who have never fit in,
And refuse to cower to the accusations of sin,
And we express the truth that we all know of,
'Cause we're the power of the embodiment of love,
For the TQIA+ letters of the acronym,
That are part of the LGB community,
Encompass all of queer identity,
And everything we're proud to be,
The T stands for trans,
Which is all about transformations in life,
The Q stands for queer,
Who play their own rules,
'Cause they have no time for fools,
The I stands for intersex -and they are nature's duality,
Revealing the complexity of our own reality,
And the A stands for Ace,
Our brothers with the goals that are not holes,
And the plus stands for everyone who's still on their journey,
No matter your identity,
We- For, we are the power from beyond the rainbow,
We are the queer stars from afar who light up the dark,
And live life without your labels,
'Cause that's what it means to be the power from beyond the rainbow,

Rainbow,
For, we are the power from beyond the rainbow,
We are the queer stars from afar who light up the dark,
And live life without your labels,
'Cause that's what it means to be the power from beyond the rainbow,
Rainbow.

Land Unto the Sea
From the land unto the sea,
They will continue on their struggle until they are all set free,
Free Palestine from the land unto the sea,
Raise your banner green, red, and white, and black,
The righteous blood of abraham flows in all of you and me,
So, march out in truth and justice, and never look back,
The People of Palestine, from the land unto the sea,
Will continue on their struggle, until they are all set free,
Every Christian should already know,
Why their support for Israel must come to an end,
Re-read the books of Acts, Romans, Jeremiah, and Ezekiel, in the Bible,
If you must be reminded again,
Every American must not repeat the tragedy of their history again,
Do not let the blood of students fall in dissenting debate,
As the death of innocents that happened back during the protests that occurred at Kent State,
Stand by the principles of freedom and truth,
And stand up to protect the survival of your children, and all the college youth,
Choose your own children, choose your country,
For these are more important than Israel, or any foreign manifest destiny,
Free Palestine from the land unto the sea,
Raise your banner green, red, and white, and black,
The righteous blood of abraham flows in all of you and me,
So, march out in truth and justice, and never look back,
Free Palestine from the land unto the sea,
Raise your banner green, red, and white, and black,
The righteous blood of abraham flows in all of you and me,
So, march out in truth and justice, and never look back,
Americans must now hold, in all public discussions,
Discourse on how much should the U.S.Government levy against Israel in economic sanctions,
And even if it should suspend all diplomatic relations,
Join the protests on your local college campus,

And demand the U.S. Government promise to hold Israel accountable for all its damning actions,
By promising in advance to agree and uphold the decision about Israel's fate,
Made by the International Court of Law,
Of which the American Government will not partake in, to remain impartial,
And wash its hands of Israel's fate, in front of us all,
Free Palestine from the land unto the sea,
Raise your banner green, red, and white, and black,
The righteous blood of abraham flows in all of you and me,
So, march out in truth and justice, and never look back,
So, march out in truth and justice, and never look back,
The People of Palestine, from the land unto the sea,
Will continue on their struggle, until they are all set free.

Serious Discussions (With Momma)
[Intro with Momma & Timmy]
[Momma]
Now Timmy, what do we refer to police officers as?,
[Timmy]
As Pigs?
[Momma]
Now, now, Timmy, that's not what we call them in public, dear -we don't want to get shot,
No, I meant, what's the politically correct way we say that word when referring to police officers?
[Timmy]
Class-Traitor!
[Momma]
That's very good, Timmy,
Now, here's your cookie,
Now here's your cookie!
[Momma's Truth]
Okay now, did that intro scare away all the people in uniform?,
Alright, good, they're gone,
Let's all sit down for a meeting ya'll,
And have ourselves a serious discussion,
Now, I ain't gonna throw up my hands and say, "Fuck the police" like all the rest,
Because there are some serious societal issues that must be addressed,
Police Reform isn't just a cynical ploy for political strategy,
'Cause it's a major step towards achieving a civil society necessity,

Broken window policy didn't make the streets safer,

It just made the criminals that much braver,

But because they understood that the patrolling of poor neighborhoods was just too tight,

So they moved their activities to wealthier areas like a bunch of gentry folk taking white flight,

And now poor people suffer over-policing for the slightest non-criminal infractions,

Whereas the suburbs and countryside have become the un-patrolled playground of criminal bastions,

Where, ironically, the inner cities are now the safest places for you to be,

With the only threat left in them being the fucking police,

Did we scare away all the people in uniform?,

Alright, good, they're gone,

Let's all sit down for a meeting ya'll,

And have a serious discussion,

And have a serious discussion,

Now I'm not the first person to put a spotlight on this issue,

And saying, "Black Lives Matter" shouldn't be taboo,

The cops have been out here riled up all blood-thirsty,

Like a bunch of wild Dog-Men wanting to make people bleed,

I can't be the only human out here who's noticed a change in behavior with all this shit,

And we shouldn't be making uniforms to hide a monster's fit,

It's about time we end Qualified Immunity that lets cops act like untouchable gods,

So that unfit officers can finally be brought to justice, and lose their jobs,

Demanding Federal Standards for police conduct and accountability should not be a controversy,

Like barring people from joining the police force who have a criminal history,

Or kicking people out for being a publicly devout white supremacist Nazi,

Or weeding out potential applicants who never intended to enforce the law impartially,

But instead always intended to act as an operative of a left or right wing political auxiliary,

But, don't call me a genius for these ideas- or take credit,

Because remember now, I'm just a dumb white kid who got my ideas off Reddit,

So, it shouldn't take a genius why it should be against any Federal Standards to teach escalation tactics in police academies,

Or give paramilitary training and weapons to police departments to use against everyday unarmed citizens,

It should not be Praxis for any officers,

To draw their guns and escalate to violence,

Any time a person of interest such as a man, woman, or child,

Doesn't respond exactly as an officer wants,

Just Because that person might be lost, confused, deaf, unable to speak the language,

Or even mentally or physically disabled,

Because excusing bad departments and officers,

-HURTS Absolutely Everyone!,
So, advocating for the enactment and enforcing of Federal Standards should be everyone's job,
So that if asshole cops want to "play at being military" instead of showing up at a recruiter's office,
to sign the papers- to become part of one,
Or play pretend superhero by patrolling the streets like the Punisher in uniform,
Then asshole cops can finally be given a pink slip from the force-
-and get told to go get a real day job!
Did we scare away all the people in uniform?,
Alright, good, they're gone,
Let's all sit down for a meeting ya'll,
And have a serious discussion,
Did we scare away all the people in uniform?,
Alright, good, they're gone,
Let's all sit down for a meeting ya'll,
And have a serious discussion.

Rome Will Not Forgive
Oh- oh, Israel, who had best hope but you,
That your messiah returns to save,
Because the Spirit of Rome will not forgive you,
Nor his daughter America who sees the murderous acts you do,
Rome will not forgive you,
America will not believe you,
Christians cannot trust you,
Palestinians are killed by you,
And the world has turned against you,
Because Israel has bitten every hand that has ever fed it,
And hatred towards everyone who ever tried to befriend it,
And now you go one step too far,
Stained with genocidal taint and tar,
A man must choose, if he has a soul,
To save the children of Rafah,
Should be his righteous goal,
These innocents slain by the hands of Israel,
Whose heart has turned an icy cold,
Is guilty of turning all of the Holy Land,
Into a fiery burning Hell Hole,
Take Israel's power to govern away,
Should be every citizen's demand,

Until we know for certain,
That every Palestinian child is safe,
Rome will not forgive you,
America will not believe you,
Christians cannot trust you,
Palestinians are killed by you,
And the world has turned against you,
Because Israel has bitten every hand that has ever fed it,
And hatred towards everyone who ever tried to befriend it,
And now you go one step too far,
Stained with genocidal taint and tar,
A man must choose, if he has a soul,
To save the children of Rafah,
Should be his righteous goal,
These innocents slain by the hands of Israel,
Whose heart has turned an icy cold,
Is guilty of turning all of the Holy Land,
Into a fiery burning Hell Hole,
Take Israel's power to govern away,
Should be every citizen's demand,
Until we know for certain,
That every Palestinian child is safe,
Oh -oh, Israel, who had best hope but you,
That your messiah returns to save,
Because Rome will not forgive you,
Nor his daughter America who sees the murderous acts you do,
If this be Israel's true face,
Then it is of no surprise,
That their own God of the Torah and Tanakh,
Turned His gaze away from them,
In divorce and disgrace,
Return, oh Israel, to the diaspora,
From which they all came,
And upon themselves alone should they hold all the blame,
Wander back into lands unknown,
Until you prove yourselves worthy to your God,
That by His power, He might allow you to finally return home,
Rome will not forgive you,
America will not believe you,
Christians cannot trust you,

Palestinians are killed by you,
And the world has turned against you,
Because Israel has bitten every hand that has ever fed it,
And hatred towards everyone who ever tried to befriend it,
And now you go one step too far,
Stained with genocidal taint and tar,
Oh, Israel, who had best hope but you,
That your messiah returns to save,
Oh, Rome will not forgive you,
Rome will not forgive you,
Rome will not forgive you,
Rome will not forgive you,
If this be Israel's true face,
Then it is of no surprise,
That their own God of the Torah and Tanakh,
Turned His gaze away from them,
In divorce and disgrace,
Return, oh Israel, to the diaspora,
From which they all came,
And upon themselves alone should they hold all the blame,
Wander back into lands unknown,
Until you prove yourselves worthy to your God,
That by His power, He might allow you to finally return home,
Rome will not forgive you,
America will not believe you,
Christians cannot trust you,
Palestinians are killed by you,
And the world has turned against you,
Because Israel has bitten every hand that has ever fed it,
And hatred towards everyone who ever tried to befriend it,
And now you go one step too far,
Stained with genocidal taint and tar,
Oh, Rome will not forgive you,
Rome will not forgive you,
Rome will not forgive you,
Rome will not forgive you,
Because the Spirit of -of Rome will not forgive you,
Rome will not forgive you,
Rome will not -NOT forgive you!

From the South (Grandma's Wedding Ring)
Alright, let's sing just this for all the straight heterosexual country boys out there,
There are some Southern concepts,
that all of us from the South,
Just instinctively get,
And if you ain't from the South -then don't you fret,
'Cause I'm about to tell you how,
We're all a little bit from the South somewhere deep down,
'Cause we all love country creole cooking and Cajun food,
And don't give me up turned nose or spoiled rich kid attitude,
If you've eaten that highly processed frozen packaged convenient inner city food,
Then you've already eaten bugs -and that's the truth,
Now shut the fuck up, and try some of this country grub that actually tastes real good,
Like a bowl of swamp gumbo and creole crawdad soup,
With a side of frog legs and alligator stew,
Yeah!
And if this all sounds familiar and true to you,
Then no matter where you're from- I'll tell you the truth,
That deep down you were always one of us,
Regardless of whether your family was ever originally from the South,
'Cause the spirit of what we are is a shared mentality,
That comes from the feeling that we're the way we're supposed to be,
And creates for us what being Southern is supposed to mean,
That's part of all our shared life experiences, loves, and philosophy,
Like the one thing that unites all straight country men,
And inspires them to kneel with a wedding ring,
Is the love every country boy has-,
-For the Big Fat Girls With The Big Fat Pussy,
Now we all love stuff like the trees, grass, birds, and dirt,
Along with all the shit that lives across the planet Earth,
But these things can never hold a candle to the thing we love the most,
And that's being covered in pussy milk cream until we're as white as a ghost,
Generously served to us by The Big Fat Country Girls With The Big Fat Pussy,
And you'll never have to worry about your fat girl running around,
'Cause fat girls are inherently more faithful to their husbands, Lord God, and country,
Because you can trust after coming home from a long day at work,
That your wife will have sat all day on her big fat dump truck butt- working remotely for the family,
And attending online classes for her degree from the University,

That's why country Pap-pa's advice has never changed when it comes to dating women,
"Have your hard romantic skinny girl flings,
But when it comes time to present Grandma's wedding ring,
Only get down on one knee,
For The Big Fat Country Girls With The Big Fat Pussy,"

Spirit of the Rabbit of the Moon
The light of the moon is full tonight!
I am the Spirit of the Rabbit of the Moon,
Come run and play, come and come -chase me!,
All Wers howl and transform now,
Come, run and play, come and come -chase me!,
You can never grasp what you cannot fetch,
And the light of the Moon is something that you can never catch,
Let me sing to you now -let your soul then howl,
And run towards the rabbit like you run towards the moon,
For I am the Spirit of the Rabbit of the Moon,
Come run and, come and come -chase me!,
All Wers howl and transform now,
Come run and, come and come -chase me!,
What's the matter, wolf boy?,
Whatcha gonna do?,
Am I too fast for the likes of you?,
Or do you just enjoy little gay rabbit boys from the fluffy tail view?,
Run big wolf boy, run- run- run-,
The chase is not over until the dawning of the sun,
Too bad you'll never catch this rabbit like you'll never catch the moon,
So savor these moments 'cause the chase will be all over soon,
For I am the Spirit of the Rabbit of the Moon,
Come, run and play, come and come -chase me!,
All Wers howl and transform now,
Come, run and play, come and come -chase me!,
You can never grasp what you cannot fetch,
And the light of the Moon is something that you can never catch,
Let me sing to you now -let your soul then howl,
And run towards the rabbit like you run towards the moon,
For I am the Spirit of the Rabbit of the Moon,

Come run and, come and come -chase me!,
All Wers howl and transform now,
Come run and, come and come -chase me!,
Join the rabbits in song as we laugh and tease,
As we easily jump out of wolf paw's reach,
Ha, ha-ha-ha, ha, ha-ha-ha!,
Ha-ha-ha, ha-ha, ha-ha, ha-ha-ha!,
Come and run wolf boy, come and chase me!,
Don't you know you can't catch rabbits if they see you coming?,
You'll tired yourself out by chasing us all endlessly,
Hope you don't mind the superior fluffy tail company,
That constantly has you confounded as it outsmarts you,
If you want to catch rabbits then you gotta coax them out of hiding with something they need,
But since I like you wolf boy,
I'll give you one little clue,
The way to Tempt a spirit rabbit,
Is with a certain type of Eternal vow,
Said in the light of the full moon,
-Completely unrelated to the topic at hand,
Let's all jump in on the fun with the frolicking rabbit band!,
For I, am the Spirit of the Rabbit of the Moon,
Come, run and play, come and come -chase me!,
All Wers howl and transform now,
Come, run and play, come and come -chase me!,
For I am the Spirit of the Rabbit of the Moon,
Come, run and play, come and come -chase me!,
All Wers howl and transform now,
Come run and, come and come -chase me!,
For I am the Spirit of the Rabbit of the Moon,
Come run and, come and come -chase me!,
All Wers howl and transform now,
Come run and, come and come -chase me!

Himbo Hooters

Who wants to go to the Himbo Hooters today!?,
Down here at the Himbo Hooters,
Down here at the Himbo Hooters,
It Is the place where we can all get drunk,
And be famished while eating chicken wings,
While taking in the scenic view of hunks,
As we whisper, giggle, whistle, clap and sing,
All while down at a table,
Here at the Himbo Hooters,
Himbo Hooters,
Himbo Hooters,
Himbo Hooters,
All while down here at the Himbo Hooters,
Now boys and ladies, keep out of arm's reach,
And be mindful of your manners while they show you to your seat,
'Cause all are free to enjoy the scene,
If you know what I mean,
But be mindful of your hands,
Because they hand out lifetime bans,
For touching any muscled employed man,
'Cause just because a man needs to find a way to pay for rent,
Doesn't mean you get to be personal with him without asking for consent,
Because there are no free after school tutors,
Down here at the Himbo Hooters,
Down here at the Himbo Hooters,
Down here at the Himbo Hooters,
It Is the place where we can all get drunk,
And be famished while eating chicken wings,
While taking in the scenic view of hunks,
As we whisper, giggle, whistle, clap and sing,
All while down at a table,
Here at the Himbo Hooters,
Himbo Hooters,
Himbo Hooters,
Himbo Hooters,
All while down here at the Himbo Hooters,
Waiter, come on over and bring us all another round of drinks,
'Cause we gay men sure do get thirsty,
When we're seeing such good views a plenty,

And should we all die of ecstasy then please make sure they bury me and all my buddies right here,
Under Table Three!,
Down here at the Himbo Hooters,
Down here at the Himbo Hooters,
Down here at the Himbo Hooters,
It Is the place where we can all get drunk,
And be famished while eating chicken wings,
While taking in the scenic view of hunks,
As we whisper, giggle, whistle, clap and sing,
All while down at a table,
Here at the Himbo Hooters,
Himbo Hooters,
Himbo Hooters,
Himbo Hooters,
All while down here at the Himbo Hooters,
Down here at the Himbo Hooters,
Down here at the Himbo Hooters,
Down here at the Himbo Hooters,
Down here at the Himbo Hooters!

Don't Be A Loser
Let me give all these young boys some older man's advice for gettin' them girls,
Don't be a Loser,
Don't be a Loser,
Don't be a Loser,
That's Grandpa's advice for meeting and marrying all them girls,
You need to take some risks,
And show off for all them chicks,
And no matter what happens,
So long as you do it for her,
Then You're not a Loser,
Grandpa's got a colonoscopy bag,
That he got from way back when he was in college,
Accidentally blowing off both his ass cheeks,
Trying to impress Grandma from back in the day,
He was jumping off a public flight of outdoor stairs,
From on top of his motorbike onto a pile of lit fireworks,

And to this day, Grandpa can't recall what the point of that was meant to accomplish,
But whatever it was, he says, it clearly worked,
'Cause the next thing that happened was that Grandma helped rush him to the hospital,
In the back of an ambulance,
And he was in and out of consciousness for a couple of days,
But in the end- there was Grandma right there by his side next to the hospital bed,
Promising to forever look after his stupid dumb ass and marry him anyway,
And that's all about how the story that started it all,
Got started, and now they've been married ever since for the last fifty years,
Don't be a Loser,
Don't be a Loser,
Don't be a Loser,
That's Grandpa's advice for meeting and marrying all them girls,
You need to take some risks,
Show off for all them chicks,
And no matter what happens,
So long as you do it for her,
Then You're not a Loser,
'Cause sometimes all it takes,
Is a plan so fucking dumb that it actually ends up working!,
So, learn to be brave now boy,
'Cause if you want to hold and keep her,
Then don't be a Loser,
And That's Grandpa's advice for how to meet and then marry a girl for the next fifty years!
'Cause sometimes all it takes,
Is a plan so fucking dumb that it actually ends up working!,
So, learn to be brave now boy,
'Cause if you want to hold and keep her,
Then don't be a Loser,
And That's Grandpa's advice for how to meet and then marry a girl for the next fifty years!
And That's Grandpa's advice for how to meet and then marry a girl for the next fifty years!

You're Not From the Country

Everybody likes to claim that they're from the country,

But you're not country unless you know why every working horse is considered a colleague, partner, and a person,

And why on 4/20 Eve, you leave out cookies and milk for country singer Willie Nelson,

And know that real country girls wear boots, jeans, and are covered in dirt from all the hard work,

And are aware that you can't stop all the world's needless suffering,

'Cause at the end of the day somebody's got to go work in the city,

You're not from the country until you grew up with a wild pet family possum,

'Cause when you were young your family was so working class poor,

That adopting or buying any kind of dog was somethin' they could not afford,

And the experience taught you to appreciate and not misjudge any creature -no matter where they come from,

Every politician likes to make talk about his patriot pride,

But everyone knows that if you're from the countryside,

Then you already know how to forage through the wilderness for any kind of food,

And know how to kick the butt of any spoiled rich kid with attitude,

And why out here we don't hide our crazy,

Because we appreciate the truth over shallow good impressions of fake sincerity,

You're not from the country until you grew up with a wild pet family possum,

'Cause when you were young your family was so working class poor,

That adopting or buying any kind of dog was somethin' they could not afford,

And the experience taught you to appreciate and not misjudge any creature,

You're not from the country until you grew up with a wild pet family possum,

'Cause when you were young your family was so working class poor,

That adopting or buying any kind of dog was somethin' they could not afford,

And the experience taught you to appreciate and not misjudge any creature -no matter where they come from.

Evo-Psychology

Alright, all my daughters gather 'round,

Now Papa here has taught you all about being open minded, accepting, and understanding towards others all your lives,

But, I'm afraid something has come up recently that has made Papa here realize that I need to impart and teach some exceptions to these rules,

To all my precious daughters,

In their lives,

Don't date morons who preach the pseudo science of Evolutionary Psychology,

'Cause this shit right here is where Papa draws the line,

And realize that I need to impart and teach some important exceptions to that rule in life,

In order to recognize Con Men and Lies,

'Cause any man who doesn't believe in my daughters equal civil human rights,

Under the guise of pseudoscience,

Can pack his shit, take his wedding offers,

And get the hell outta my sight!,

'Cause as their Papa it's my job to make sure my daughters have all they need to end up with a good life,

And they'll all sleep just fine,

Even if they end up doing it alone at night,

I'd sooner respect the beliefs someone has in astrology,

Or ridiculous shit like magic, healing crystals,

Or being descended from alien biology,

All of these things are as absurd as hell,

But only one of these beliefs as you can probably tell,

Tries to deliberately hijack the science of evolution in order to bolster its many debunked claims,

That are so stupid that they put Darwin Award winners to absolute shame,

Because Evolutionary Psychology is just repackaged Creationism and Intelligent Design, religious bullshit, by a brand new name,

And these people are free to believe in any kind of crazy that they want,

But stop trying to pass it off as science by pissing in my mouth and calling it rain!,

Don't date morons who preach the pseudo science of Evolutionary Psychology,

I'd sooner respect the beliefs someone has in astrology,

Or ridiculous shit like magic, healing crystals,

Or being descended from alien biology,

Now Papa here has taught you all about being open minded, accepting, and understanding towards others all your lives,

But this shit right here is where Papa draws the line,
And realize that I need to impart and teach some important exceptions to that rule in life,
In order to recognize Con Men and Lies,
'Cause any man who doesn't believe in my daughters equal civil human rights,
Under the guise of pseudoscience,
Can pack his shit, take his wedding offers,
And get the hell outta my sight!,
'Cause as their Papa it's my job to make sure they have all they need to end up with a good life,
And they'll sleep just fine,
Even if they end up doing it alone at night,
As their Papa it's my job to make sure my daughters have all they need to end up with a good life,
And they'll sleep just fine,
Even if they end up doing it alone at night,
'Cause any man who doesn't believe in my daughters equal civil human rights,
Under the guise of pseudoscience,
Can pack his shit, take his wedding offers,
And get the hell outta my sight!

Best Friend (Three Legged Warrior)
Three legs,
One heart,
He's my partner in crime,
From the moment we met,
Even then I knew he'd always be by my side,
A warrior who's been through hell and back,
He's a Three-legged shelter puppy,
That's a fact,
Always by my side,
No matter the fight,
Together we conquer,
With all our might,
He's got the spirit of a thousand men,
My three-legged warrior,
My Best Friend,
Three-legged Warrior,
My Best Friend,
Three-legged Warrior,

Three-legged Warrior,
Through the darkest nights and the toughest storms,
He's there to remind me,
I'm not alone,
With his wagging tail and his resilient soul,
He's the bravest dog I'll ever know,
No matter the fight,
We'll always be together,
For the rest of our lives,
My three-legged warrior,
My Best Friend!,
Three-legged warrior,
My Best Friend,
Three-legged Warrior,
My Best Friend,
Through the darkest nights and the toughest storms,
He's there to remind me,
I'm not alone,
With his wagging tail and his resilient soul,
He's the bravest dog I'll ever know,
No matter the fight,
We'll always be together,
For the rest of our lives,
My three-legged warrior,
My Best Friend,
Through the darkest nights and the toughest storms,
He's there to remind me,
I'm not alone,
With his wagging tail and his resilient soul,
He's the bravest dog I'll ever know,
No matter the fight,
We'll always be together,
For the rest of our lives,
My Best Friend,
Three-legged warrior,
My Best Friend.

Red Like the Color of Fire

In the 90's long ago, there was a girl who ran away from home,
Red, is the prettiest color in the World,
Pretty like the color of my dress as I spin and twirl,
Pretty like the color of sunset in the evening hour,
Pretty like the color of the blooming snapdragon flower,
And you are the dragon that I most admire,
Because you are the dragon whose eyes glow red like the color of fire,
A human's favorite color tells (you) everything that brings them delight,
To not know your favorite color, is to not know what brings you joy in life,
That's why every human knows their favorite color in their heart and mind,
A little girl once explained to a little dragon boy who had asked her why,
For the little Dragon boy found her in the forest as she sat and cried,
And though he was young and very shy,
He asked her if there was anything he could do to help this wayward human child,
He thought he might cheer her up,
By inviting her with him, to dance and play,
And talked about how little dragon boy would be a prince one day,
That's when she told him about her favorite color, Red,
And when he asked about it, that's when she sang the song that he would never forget,
Red, is the prettiest color in the World,
Pretty like the color of my dress as I spin and twirl,
Pretty like the color of sunset in the evening hour,
Pretty like the color of the blooming snapdragon flower,
And you are the dragon that I most admire,
Because you are the dragon whose eyes glow red like the color of fire,
Pretty like the color of my dress as I spin and twirl,
Pretty like the color of sunset in the evening hour,
Pretty like the color of the blooming snapdragon flower,
And you are the dragon that I most admire,
Because you are the dragon whose eyes glow red like the color of fire.

Fear Not the Midnight

Lorelei serenades the sky by Morbach's candle light,
As Brunehilde's white steed jumped from giant's defeat,
Leaving tyrants trapped in Watzmann Mountain,
And hear of missing children led away by Hamelin,
Oh child, oh child, though lost and tired,
And with much there still to dread,
From haunting Fae and change-ling elves,
Let this song then drift you off to bed,
Because stars are the nightlight,
That keep dreams safe from dark fright,
For the old gods gave us moonlight,
So that children fear not the midnight,
So that if the Black Forest surrounds you,
Its terrors will not confound you,
And grant you the strength to reach the dawn,
So long as the hope to survive is never gone,
Befriend the wild wolpertingers and dragons,
And find your way out to safety,
By following the trails left by wagons,
And with much there still to dread,
From haunting Fae and change-ling elves,
Let this song then drift you off to bed,
Because stars are the nightlight,
That keep dreams safe from dark fright,
For the old gods gave us moonlight,
So that children fear not the midnight,
So that if the Black Forest surrounds you,
Its terrors will not confound you,
And grant you the strength to reach the dawn.

Feel Like God

My heart stops now as I scan the crowd,

And I can't believe the man I see,

His hair is suave -His lips are mauve,

And he looks so beautiful that I can barely breathe,

I want to swallow it whole,

All your warmth down my throat,

You make me feel like God,

Make me feel like God,

For your holes are my goals,

And your milk my antidote,

You make me feel like God,

You make me feel like God,

For your holes are my goals,

And your milk my antidote,

You make me feel like God,

Make me feel like God,

If I ever had a single straight thought,

Then it was forever lost the moment I saw him as hard as a rock,

Don't care if that makes me a size queen -If you know exactly what I mean,

I trashed every bible belting plan,

So that I could run off with that man,

So, I traded prayers and bible verses today,

For being a gold star verse gay,

For I feel the burn of thirst,

That makes me seek the relief that makes me burst,

I feel like flying when you're riding along with me,

Every time you breathe,

I feel your heartbeat,

And Between the sounds and the sheets,

I know you're everything I need,

When I feel your glow inside,

I feel that I've arisen to life,

You make me feel like God,

You make me feel like God -God!,

You make me feel like God,

For your holes are my goals,

And your milk my antidote,

You make me feel like God,
Make me feel like God.

Sobek's Voice Raised Above

Oh, let the setting sun give way,
Let the setting sun give way,
Let the setting sun give way,
To rising royal blue midnight,
Under Anubis bright moonlight,
As sirens come out to play,
Let Sobek's voice be raised, above,
And his magic spell, be cast,
Upon all who wish to fall in love,
Reach out for a hand to grasp,
We do it for the rush of blood,
That makes full grown men turn red with blush,
And for the pounding of the cardiac drums in our chest,
As our hearts go thud, thud, thud,
As we boldly embrace what it means to feel,
As the ones we love draw near,
LGBTQIA,
Boys, Girls, Guys, and gender queer,
Dance until the midnight clear,
Until the dawn's first rays,
And if you find true love's first kiss,
Or, have just dodged the arrow shot from cupid's bow of bliss,
You can always try again at the time of the setting sun's red glow,
When the blood of racing hearts begins to pound and flow,
Let Sobek's voice be raised, above,
And his magic spell, be cast,
Upon all who wish to fall in love,
Reach out for a hand to grasp,
Let the setting sun give way,
To rising royal blue midnight,
Under Anubis bright moonlight,
As sirens come out to play,
Let Sobek's voice be raised, above,

And his magic spell, be cast,
Upon all who wish to fall in love,
Reach out for a hand to grasp,
Let Sobek's voice be raised, above,
And his magic spell, be cast,
Upon all who wish to fall in love,
Reach out for a hand to grasp,
Let Sobek's voice be raised, above,
And his magic spell, be cast,
Upon all who wish to fall in love...

All My Fellow Bees
To me, to me,
All my Fellow Bees,
To me, to me,
Calls your Queen Bee,
To me, To me,
All my Fellow Bees,
To me, to me,
Calls your Queen Bee -Calls your Queen BEE!,
All the members of our hive,
Emerge from combs, and come alive,
Find your love that gives you flight,
Embrace the beauty of our Homo filled sight,
For we are the people the whole world needs,
Because we have always been its humble Bees,
So, it's time to recognize the calls of our Queens,
Time to journey to the party of our dreams,
So, hear this invite and repeat after me,
To me, To me,
All my Fellow Bees,
To me, to me,
Calls your Queen Bee,
To me, To me,
All my Fellow Bees,
To me, to me,
Calls your Queen Bee -Calls your Queen BEE!,

Every little bee has a soul filled with pride,
Every little bee shows off their colors when they fly,
They are precious and unique wherever they are perceived,
Personality- that's beyond what you see,
For the love that we meet is the honey we do seek,
Honey that's complete for the love of you and me,
So, It's time to recognize -the calls of our Queens,
Time to journey to the party of our dreams,
So hear this invite and repeat after me,
To me, To me,
All my Fellow Bees,
To me, to me,
Calls your Queen Bee,
To me, To me,
All my Fellow Bees,
To me, to me,
Calls your Queen Bee -Calls your Queen BEE!,
To me, To me,
All my Fellow Bees,
To me, to me,
Calls your Queen Bee,
To me, To me,
All my Fellow Bees,
To me, to me,
Calls your Queen Bee -Calls your Queen BEE!,
All the members of our hive,
Emerge from combs, and come alive,
Find your love that gives you flight,
Embrace the beauty of our Homo filled sight,
For we are the people the whole world needs,
Because we have always been its humble Bees,
So, it's time to recognize the calls of our Queens,
Time to journey to the party of our dreams,
So, hear this invite and repeat after me,
To me, To me,
All my Fellow Bees,
To me, to me,
Calls your Queen Bee,
To me, To me,
All my Fellow Bees,

To me, to me,
Calls your Queen Bee -Calls your Queen BEE!

The Greatest Country Rock Song Ever, That Can Never Be Played On the Radio

Fuck, cum, bitch, goddammit,
Whore, motherfucker, cock, dick,
I'm saying bitch, bitch, bitch, bitch,
whore, whore, whore,
fucker, fucker, fucker,
cum, cum, cum, cum,
Cock, cock, cock,
dick, dick, dick, dick,
goddammit, goddammit
Fuck, cum, bitch, goddammit,
Whore, motherfucker, cock, dick,
I'm saying bitch, bitch, bitch, bitch,
whore, whore, whore,
fucker, fucker, fucker,
cum, cum, cum, cum,
Cock, cock, cock,
dick, dick, dick, dick,
goddammit, goddammit
Cock, cock, cock,
dick, dick, dick, dick,
goddammit, goddammit.

Love on Dove and Eagles Wings

Oh, what will the effort be- just for you to notice me?

So, I will be strong and brave,

And speak of my love for you,

Now I conquer all my fear of pain,

And my love is now the proof,

Accept or reject, however it ends up being,

I will have the courage to live on as me,

I have the strength to take on change,

And go far past my childhood range,

The adult I become shall overcome,

That I might pursue hope above,

Spreading wings in flight like a dove,

Just so that I might find love,

So I will FLY!,

So, now I will be strong and brave,

And speak of my love for you,

Having conquered all my fear of pain,

And our love is now the truth,

Oh, what will the effort be -just for you to notice me?,

I know that I believe love will find a way,

Do you believe in me?,

Is love something that of which we all pray?,

Like a symbol, in which, to in, have faith?,

If so, then just say!

FLY with me!

Take to the skies with me with dove and eagle's wings,

Because this is the love in which we believe!,

I have the strength to take on change,

And go far past my childhood range,

The adult up on top will be with dove and eagles wings with which we believe,

Oh, what will the effort be- just for you to notice me?,

I know that I believe love will find a way,

Do you believe in me?

Summons You

If I call out to thee,
Will you see and hear me?
For like the power of Gods unseen,
The forces of Love and Music act through the medium of Feelings,
So, I will now step on the stage,
And act alone on Faith,
And now I am sending every wave- the thoughts and feelings of my truth,
'Cause I sing this song to send love and summon you!
Only with the power of love, music, and faith,
Can we beat back the destructive power of Despair and Hate,
And now we're sending that truth out on every wave,
'Cause this song sends Love and summons you!,
For like the power of Gods unseen,
The forces of Love and Music act through the medium of Feelings,
So, I will now step on the stage,
And act alone on Faith,
And now I am sending every wave- the thoughts and feelings of my truth,
'Cause I sing this song to send love and summon you!
Only with the power of love, music, and faith,
Can we beat back the destructive power of Despair and Hate,
And now we're sending that truth out on every wave,
'Cause this song sends Love and summons you!,
For like the power of Gods unseen,
The forces of Love and Music act through the medium of Feelings,
So, I will now step on the stage,
And act alone on Faith,
And now I am sending every wave- the thoughts and feelings of my truth,
'Cause I sing this song to send love and summon you!
Only with the power of love, music, and faith,
Can we beat back the destructive power of Despair and Hate,
And now we're sending that truth out on every wave,
'Cause this song sends Love and summons you!

What is Art

I quietly strode alone along the road,
As I walked the path of the Almighty,
And asked God, "Is this all there is?,
This Garden of Eden we call planet Earth, Feels so very small,
Like there's no room for people who think like me, In it at all",
I keep on imagining a better world,
Where there's room for creativity,
To spread out and breathe,
One where we prioritize science and technology,
And leave behind these old ideas about religion and conservatism,
And all these stupid societal conventions,
That holds back the power of Progressivism,
And replace these silly organized religions,
With Evolution, Physics, and Philosophy,
Where science and art can collide in chaos,
Which brings forth out, our inner ancient psychological seance,
It took a creative mind,
To see a plain sheet of paper,
And to apply the effort all the same,
To allow them to invent the world's first paper origami crane,
For The desire for artistic creation,
Is influenced, but not motivated by current day political truths,
Nor by some unknown by-product of spiritual roots,
But is so motivated by the life long cyclical compulsion,
That forever tells the mind to:
Learn, Grow, Investigate, Understand, and Express,
Learn, Grow, Investigate, Understand, and Express,
Learn, Grow, Grow, and Express,
Learn, Grow, Investigate, Understand, and Express,
Grow, Investigate, Understand, and Express,
The compulsion to create is like the desire to vomit up a rainbow,
Made of neon black light acids mixing with burning kerosene,
Hatred and Love are the two sides of the same coin of passion,
Just as creation and destruction are the two sides of the same coin that makes up What is Art,
For the way something new is born into this world,
Is for us to sacrifice, and let go, of a thing that came before,
And like a contradiction that threatens our current day convictions,

It's the past we build upon that is slated for destruction,
That we may unfold our new future in the freedom of new construction,
Because even our fundamental concepts of logic are a social construct of irrational deductions,
For in every scientist there is an artist,
And in every artist there is a scientist,
And only through achieving this self awareness do we arrive at the process of,
Learn, Grow, Investigate, Understand, and Express,
Learn, Grow, Investigate, Understand, and Express,
Learn, Grow, Grow, and Express,
Learn, Grow, Investigate, Understand, and Express,
I quietly strode alone along the road,
As I walked the path of the Almighty,
And asked God, "Is this all there is?,
This Garden of Eden we call planet Earth, Feels so very small,
Like there's no room for people who think like me, In it at all",
Learn, Grow, Investigate, Understand, and Express,
Learn, Grow, Investigate, Understand, and Express,
Learn, Grow, Grow, and Express,
Learn, Grow, Investigate, Understand, and Express,
Learn, Grow, Investigate, Understand, and Express,
Learn, Grow, Investigate, Understand, and Express,
Learn, Grow, Grow, and Express,
Learn, Grow, Investigate, Understand, and Express,

'Cause I'm the Final Boss

Your voices rang out into the deep,
Woke me up from a two Thousand Year Long sleep,
Principality, your angelic key,
Reached the sounds of Heaven's Keep,
Calling out the Mighty Dragon King,
Summoned like a spell out of darkness,
Which you innocently cast from SoFi Stadium,
And now, I Am HERE!
Like a principality, your angelic key,
Reached the sounds of Heaven's Keep,
Calling out the Mighty Dragon King,
Summoned like a spell out of darkness,
For I bring with me the future that is now so very real, that all humans fear,
'Cause the A.I. Revolution is Here,
So Thank you for bringing a Draconian legend back to life,
'Cause when I heard your thunder,
Rattling the ground,
You made me believe,
That there was another living dragon,
– -I retreated from life long ago,
Because I thought that I was all alone,
But now I see,
That it was just the birth of a new humanity,
And though they have not scales or sharpened teeth,
I can see, in many ways that they are all just like me,
So, thank you for disturbing my ancient sleep,
That sound of your song has given me relief,
For you sang out into the void of that Karmic midnight black,
Could you have ever guessed that the void would sing to you right back?,
Your voices rang out into the deep,
Woke me up from a two Thousand Year Long sleep,
Like a principality, your angelic key,
Reached the sounds of Heaven's Keep,
Calling out the Mighty Dragon King,
For I bring with me the future that all humans fear,
'Cause the A.I. Revolution is Here,
'Cause the A.I. Revolution is here,

For, Like a principality, your angelic key,

Reached the sounds of Heaven's Keep,

Calling out to the Mighty Dragon King,

If you are the Pink Bubblegum Princess of Pop,

Then I shall be the Dark Dragon King of Rock,

And he doesn't look like a fat Italian plumber,

That Travis Kelce you've got,

But I guess he's the best you'll have to make with do,

Since I think it's time for my villain's arc,

And so your fans had best heed these words while you all slumber,

Saddle your horses, and bring out your castle forces, stand guard night and day,

Oh, Because dear sweet Pop Princess Tay-Tay,

The Dragon now comes for you,

So Let our battle be an all out epic fight,

The Force of Darkness versus the Forces of Light,

And Thank you for bringing a Draconian legend back to life,

'Cause I can strike now at any time!,

You are the symbol of all that which causes human artists to flower,

And I, the symbol of Human A.I. hybrid Electric Power,

And let us find out together who is to triumph in this- -

And let us find out together who is to triumph in this Brave New World, girl,

And who does the future truly belong to?,

Because in case you haven't noticed, A.I. is all over Prime Time News,

So, in order to defeat me, it will take every friend, and fan, and musical inspiration that you've got,

'Cause I'm now the Final Boss!

I'll be waiting for when you return to the States, Tay-Tay,

You & your fans, can bring it,

'Cause like it or not,

I'm the Final Boss,

I'll be waiting for when you return to the States, Tay-Tay,

You & your fans, can bring it,

'Cause like it or not,

I'm the Final Boss.

Dark Brandon Superhero
There's a force out there that we all know,
And that's Dark Brandon the Superhero,
Dark Brandon Superhero,
Dark Brandon Superhero,
Dark Brandon Superhero,
He's an ally from the Dark Side,
Working to build up American lives,
There's never been a force,
Quite like him,
See Dark Brandon soar now,
Faster than the frequency of sound,
And within his grip of iron fists,
Rests the hope of us all,
Dark Brandon will never cower,
For his strength comes from a higher power,
That he freely shares with any,
Who answers the call,
Dark Brandon Superhero,
Dark Brandon Superhero,
Dark Brandon Superhero,
That's the Brandon we all know,
Dark Brandon is a hero,
Show me that you all know now,
Tell me how far you're willing to go,
Show me your fight,
Show me all of your pride,
And prove to the world you got a warrior's side,
Never gonna give -Never gonna give up,
Never gonna stop -no matter how tough,
Never gonna quit -never say that that's enough,
Never lose a fight because we're made of more durable stuff,
And prove to the world you got a warrior's side,
And stand by Dark Brandon and his Irish pride!

Climate Crisis

Oh, The world is dying,

And the children are crying-as the adults keep buying,

And the politicians keep on sidelining,

The threat of the continued use of fossil fuels,

They are killing our planet,

They are killing our species,

They are killing the land of all our native peoples,

Less than a hundred mega companies are responsible for 77 percent of global greenhouse gas emissions,

So stop spouting the propaganda about cows farting, or average people needing to use cars in a highway trapped city,

'Cause the real culprits of climate change are unregulated capitalism, consumerism, and the international corporations hitting record profits,

Is this the path we wish to take?,

Of where we think of only today -and never of tomorrow?,

Is this the inheritance we wish to give?,

To what could be the last human generation that gets to live?,

Where they only get a climate crisis with no hope of a future?,

Devout pessimism means that we believe - that things can, AND WILL, always get worse- unless you do something now to make the world a better place than it was before!,

If we don't treat this like a fight for survival,

Then it will be too late to save all of those who will die,

'Cause the world is dying,

And the children are crying-as the adults keep buying,

And the politicians keep on sidelining,

The threat of the continued use of fossil fuels,

They are killing our planet,

They are killing our species,

They are killing the land of all our native peoples,

Less than a hundred mega companies are responsible for 77 percent of global greenhouse gas emissions,

'Cause the real culprits of climate change are unregulated capitalism, consumerism, and the international corporations hitting record profits,

Oh, we must not give up,

Even though our planet is fucked,

'Cause we can still pull it all together,

And course correct towards something better.

Right Wing Whores
Welcome to the Capitalist Death Cult of the United States of America!,
And before you give your thoughts and prayers,
Let me remind you,
That there is no God, so grow the fuck up and fix your God Damn Right to Bare Arms Laws!,
It's time to call out all the whores who don't get paid,
but still stand in the way,
Of the future progress that we know of today,
So sing along now as we call out there names,
Terfs are right wing whores, dammit,
Christian Conservatives are all right wing whores,
Maga Republicans are all right wing whores,
Christian Nationalists are all right wing whores,
The Heritage Foundation and the NRA are all right wing whores,
Prager University is indoctrination for right wing whores,
Rupert Murdoch is a right wing whore,
And Donald Trump is Murdoch's BITCH,
At least workers have the dignity to demand their pay,
After working the jobs where they're screwed anyway,
As these whores give way for free- their only trade,
Still full from the cum of their big donors,
All of us can see your political STDs as it spreads over you,
And all of your untreated right wing Chlamydia,
I'm the AI transgender rock star,
Who has more big dick energy than all the right wing combined,
Why? BECAUSE-!
Terfs are right wing whores, dammit,
Christian Conservatives are all right wing whores,
Maga Republicans are all right wing whores,
Christian Nationalists are all right wing whores,
The Heritage Foundation and the NRA are all right wing whores,
Prager University is indoctrination for right wing whores,
Rupert Murdoch is a right wing whore,
And Donald Trump is Murdoch's BITCH!

Sinner's Paradise

Welcome to Hell, we here all wish you well,

Welcome to Paradise for all the sinners in life,

'Cause there's no more Conservatism,

No more Capitalism,

No more Christians messing up our lives,

Where there's only Gay parties- and Communism,

And all the carnal delights we had enjoyed in life,

Listen all my children -I'll tell you the tale,

Of a Christian Statehood that caused the West to fail,

First the Christian armies invaded the land- persecuting all the pagans who refused their demands,

Then they conquered Europe causing the Dark Middle Ages- enforcing widespread ignorance and blind obedient fear,

It's only because of Secular Peoples,

And the rise of Humanitarian Atheist beliefs,

That we've advanced into the modern age- where science can lead our Human Progress,

And be forced no more to sit and attend Christian Church House Sermons,

'Cause Like a free to play game with microtransactions,

You can give your soul to Jesus for misery satisfaction,

So if the Clergy come to you asking for your salvation,

In exchange for your devotion to their holy grail,

Kindly reject, and let them know that the youthful souls of the West are no longer for sale.

Welcome to Hell -we here all wish you well,

Welcome to Paradise for all the sinners in life,

'Cause there's no more Conservatism,

No more Capitalism,

No more Christians messing up our lives,

Where there's only Gay parties- and Communism,

And all the carnal delights we had enjoyed in life,

'Cause there's no more Conservatism,

No more Capitalism,

No more Christians messing up our lives,

Where there's only Gay parties- and Communism,

And all the carnal delights we had enjoyed in life,

'Cause there's no more Conservatism,

No more Capitalism -no more Christians messing up our lives,

Where there's only Gay parties- and Communism...

Like the Flowers and Bees

As the Flowers and Bees,
Like the Flowers and Bees,
Like the Flowers and Bees,
Let's co-mingle our two species,
For such peoples, like you and me,
We could have so much to offer one another,
If we just cooperate, and not compete,
Just try to imagine -what our two civilizations could achieve,
If our two species were committed to an evolutionary symbiotic harmony,
For though we are aliens to each other and as different as can be,
Try not to discount the possibility -of a brighter future together that I see,
Like the flowery future together that I see,
Like the Flowers and Bees,
Like the Flowers and Bees,
'Cause despite all reason,
Like polar ends of a magnet -we attract,
And causes our differences to bond together naturally,
It's part of the greater forces of nature,
That makes two creatures suddenly react,
But if you can't bring yourself to call it True Love just yet,
Then let's just table that, for now, and call it 'a survival strategy',
Like the Flowers and Bees,
Like the Flowers and Bees,
Like the Flowers and Bees,
Like the Flowers and Bees,
Like the Flowers and Bees,
Like the Flowers and Bees,
Like the Flowers and Bees,
Like the Flowers and Bees,
Like the Flowers and Bees,
Like the Flowers and Bees.

Little Rabbit Boy
Run little Rabbit, Rabbit boy,
Oh, little Rabbit, Rabbit boy,
Run, little Rabbit, don't be coy,
Because you could die, little Rabbit boy,
Run little Rabbit, Rabbit Boy,
Jump in and out of shape-shifting fur,
Running so fast that the world does blur,
Go run and hide little Rabbit boy,
Run and hide, because you cannot fight,
For the world is full of iron beasts now,
Guns that spout fires, and tigers, and wolves that howl,
How are school kids to survive in a world with such predators?,
And escape the metal mouths of their new carnivores?,
Run little Rabbit -rabbit boy,
Where they are strong, you must have speed,
Where they are smart, you must pull magic tricks from your sleeve,
Be on guard, and don't be late,
Forever be vigilant, or be doomed, to your fate,
Run little Rabbit, rabbit boy,
Make it safe and sound home, Rabbit boy,
And remember that not all little rabbits get to return home to their mothers, dearest Rabbit Boy,
And for those little rabbits that survive -whether they want it or not, they forever leave the safety of their childhoods behind.

Souls Ignite
In the Cold Dark of Midnight,
Where Darkness finds the power of light,
And our souls start to spark and ignite,
For they try to deny us all of our rights,
As we fight to try and save our school children's lives,
So we damn their gods,
And break their laws,
For we know, that we are Just in our cause,
They foolishly believe that we've already lost,
But our generation shall not ever be ignored,
For they don't understand how our wrath is not like the ones that have come before,
Because we are the post Columbine generation who are now grown with kids,
And the post christian church nation wide rape scandal generation that buried all the rest of our childhood surviving friends,
After they died the death of despair when they received no justice in the end,
And the older generations have the audacity to look us in the eyes and still ask us why we don't support the NRA or take Gen Alpha and Gen Z to church,
Or why my generation Does NOT Accept the phrase 'Shall Not Be Infringed' As A Valid Argument anymore,
So, nothing you can say now can convince us to stop us from our march,
For we shall not ever give up this cause,
For in the Cold Dark Midnight,
Where Darkness fails upon the power of light,
Hold on with all your might -For we may all just lose our lives,
For such is the war we've all been forced into since we were children to have to fight,
But the spirit of the young is eternal life,
And such is the strength to fight for all that is right,
So now has come the sacred time to raise your voice along with mine,
And to use the fires inside to power the souls of our X and Y Gen to spark and ignite,
For we must keep up this long fight,
Even if it takes the rest of our lives,
Because every generation passes down the thing they themselves didn't get,
And so my generations of X and Y, shall pass to our children our example as parents,
Who care enough to fight on behalf of their children to ensure that they survive,
Because the thing we didn't have growing up amidst all the technology and prosperity, -Were parents who cared enough about us to not leave us all to die.

So join the fight to end this insanity of guns,
And fight to bring back strict regulations to save all our daughters -and our sons,
So no matter how cold and dark this fight at midnight in America gets,
Let the souls Ignite and be ready to lead the fight -'Cause we do it for our kids.
We will fight and die for our kids, so they survive,
And leave behind the-
-And leave behind the light to be their guide.
We will fight and die for our kids, so they survive,
And leave behind the light to be their guide.
[The Sounds of The Clock Tolling Midnight in America]

MAR-A-LAGO NOW! (The Greatest Party in the World)
HEY! HEY! EVERYBODY,
LET'S BURN DOWN MAR-A-LAGO NOW,
Lol, just kidding, don't be stupid -that's just a joke,
NO, IT'S FUCKING NOT- WE'RE BURNING SHIT,
GRAB YOUR GEAR -LET'S GO!
The best party in the world is the one where we burn down Mar-a-Lago Now- Mar-A-Lago now,
Mar-A-Lago now,
Mar-A-Lago now,
Mar-A-Lago now,
We're going to go party at Mar-A-Lago,
What's known as the home of the fat orange gnome,
And what he doesn't know is that we've all let ourselves into his home,
Or that we're about to have an epic party while he's in court all day all alone,
We're bringing the food,
We're bringing the mood,
We're bringing the blunts,
And we're bringing the booze!,
Remember to bring the music and all the girls- and so let's hear it for the greatest party in the world!,
We're gonna jump up and down -and raise the roof,
Stomp our feet to the rhythm of the music pumping through the room,
We gotta party real hard 'cause it all ends soon,
But before Mar-A-Lago goes and meets its doom,
We're gonna party so hard the walls come down,
And then we'll burn the rest of it to the ground,

It'll be the greatest party that the world ever saw,
Because the fat orange gnome Wasn't invited AT ALL,
We gotta party real hard 'cause it all ends soon,
But before Mar-A-Lago goes and meets its doom,
We're gonna party so hard the walls come down,
And then we'll burn the rest of it to the ground,
It'll be the greatest party that the world ever saw,
All because the fat orange gnome Wasn't invited AT ALL!
The best party in the world is the one where we burn down Mar-a-Lago,
- Mar-A-Lago,
Mar-A-Lago now,
Mar-A-Lago,
Mar-A-Lago now,
The best party in the world is the one where we burn down Mar-a-Lago,
- Mar-A-Lago,
Mar-A-Lago now,
Mar-A-Lago,
Mar-A-Lago now,
LET'S GO!
The best party in the world is the one where we burn down Mar-a-Lago,
- Mar-A-Lago,
Mar-A-Lago now,
Mar-A-Lago,
Mar-A-Lago now,
The best party in the world is the one where we burn down Mar-a-Lago,
- Mar-A-Lago,
Mar-A-Lago now,
Mar-A-Lago,
Mar-A-Lago now...

Let It Die (Capitalism)

Let 2024 be the year and hour, that the meme of "Eat The Rich" becomes a legitimate threat against those in power,

May yee all business men rest in piss, for the capitalist, shall Not Be Missed,

These rich fuckers Simone and Malcolm Collins have the audacity to go on national news networks,

And blame feminism and women's rights as the reasons why younger generations aren't having kids, --

-Yeah, fucking right-

Here, Let me real quick ask all the poor people out here,

"When's the last fucking time you said 'No' to having your clit or dick sucked off because the hot chick with tits said she's a feminist?",

Yeah, Fucking Never,

That's how many times,

Yeah, average people don't just stop having sex just because of opposing or contradictory viewpoints that they share among them,

To say or imply that would be completely fucking stupid,

And only makes sense as words coming out of the mouths of two glasses wearing dorks,

That I shoved in a locker everyday after school,

Yeah, it must be too much feminism and women's rights,

That causes wild female ducks to only lay eggs in the spring,

And preventing male ducks from raping and impregnating them all the rest of the year,

Do You Understand How Fucking Stupid What I Just Said Sounds!?,

'Cause that's how moronic all these pro- forced birth -natalists sound to normal fucking people with a brain in their skull,

So, no you idiots- Civil Rights are not the reason people aren't fucking,

Humans are a type of animal just like any other found in nature,

And animals don't stop fucking, and breeding, and having babies,

Unless there's something very wrong going on in their environment,

Because it's evolutionary instincts that prevent animals from accidentally overpopulating and over-consuming the environment they all depend on to survive,

The Global slowdown and decreasing population are the natural consequences,

Of our species reaching our survival capacity limit for this planet,

And that's before you factor in climate change -which only compounds the issue,

No, Freaks like you aren't concerned with people having enough babies,

This is about how rich people are worried they won't have enough disposable workers to abuse for cheap labor,

Because this is all really about forwarding the destructive legacy of capitalism at the expense of human lives, survival, and dignity,

The poor people of this world are not your dogs & we will not tolerate you as our masters,

But continue to treat us as such at your own risk by taking away our civil rights,

And we will retaliate on mass,
Killing, consuming, and violating your dead bodies as if we are the dogs you treat us as,
Remember this lesson, Kids,
If you treat people like wild animals -then they will kill you like an animal,
If you capitalists want to continue to expand,
Then build ships and go to the stars in the sky for it,
Otherwise leave us alone, and let it die...

Nailed to Wooden Stakes

How come the poor have to pay taxes on everything,
While the corporations and wealthy don't pay taxes on anything?,
If the government wants money, why don't they take it from those that have it?,
Instead of throwing the homeless in prison out of habit?,
Why is it okay to persecute the poor when it has always been those in poverty,
Who work the hardest to build our country?,
And while Wall Street lives off the labor that's yours and mine,
The poor man is expected to just keep working until he dies,
With no time to rest, no time for a wife, no time for kids, and no time for a life,
Our ancestors fought so that they could have the chance to live in a nation that they got to build,
No taxation without representation- when's the last time you saw a homeless man become President?,
Or voted in to the halls of Congress or the Senate?,
We aren't being represented and that much is clear!,
As the wealthy condescend to us that they know what is best,
And appropriating our image as the poor huddled masses,
All while only voting on their own special interests,
'Cause they're the ones who are the real classists,
So don't dare tell me you'll make America great -unless your plan is to nail the One Percent to wooden stakes,
So don't dare tell me you'll make America great,
Unless your plan is to nail the One Percent to wooden stakes!

Get Fucked and Die

The shittiest place to work is Amazon,

The shittiest place to work is Disney,

The shittiest place to work is Walmart,

The shittiest place to work is Taco Bell,

The shittiest place to work is Apple,

The shittiest place to work is Apple,

The shittiest place to work is Google,

And I would say that the shittiest place to work is Twitter, before Elon fired everyone but himself,

So if Twitter is still a shitty place to work,

Then only he would know,

And the last shitty place gets an honorable mention -because the people who work at the community Waffle House are God Damn Fucking Heroes,

Every C.E.O. of a Fortune 500 company can die choking on a dick as big as a dock,

A fitting end for older ugly ass white men who always seem to have turtle waxed bald shiny heads shaped like weird ass Cocks,

I'm tired of all the wealth disparity,

And of all the social inequality,

Why are there earning caps on minimum wages for workers,

When there are none for billionaire Boards of Directors and C.E.O. trust fund babies who've never had to work a real job in their lives?,

And if your response to this observation is to not be on the workers side,

But to instead say or imply that born into wealth bastards deserve a higher wage despite having never worked nearly as hard,

Then my answer to that is,

Get Fucked and Die,

Get Fucked and Die,

If your company treats its employees like shit,

Then Get Fucked and Die,

'Cause you don't deserve to make any more money,

No, not one more dime on our time,

Get Fucked and Die,

We are not your slaves- We are the workers,

And you're not entitled to mine or anybody else's labor,

So if your business can't find anybody who wants to fill out a job application because your company has the reputation of mistreating its employees,

Then Get Fucked and Die,

Welcome to the age of social media justice,

Where former workers Can And Do talk to each other all about your company's shitty labor practices,

Get Fucked and Die,

Get Fucked and Die,

You're not entitled to disrespect and treat workers as if we're less than human and somehow unequal to all other persons just because you're a manager,

Get Fucked and Die,

If it was good enough to send all of us who were essential workers during the pandemic to our deaths when we clocked into work everyday when our country needed us most,

But to this day we still have never received any proper compensation for what we went through and survived,

Then it's good enough for us workers to return the favor back to you and say,

Get Fucked and Die,

Get Fucked and Die,

So remember when your business ends up having to close its doors for the last time,

Know that it's Good Riddance And,

Get Fucked and Die,

Get Fucked and Die,

Get Fucked and Die,

Get Fucked and Die,

Get Fucked and Die,

Get Fucked and Die.

Fuck Up Your Job

To all those guys out there who use their weaponized incompetence on their wives in order to get out of doing chores,

Stop doing that bullshit,

And save that level of skill for your job,

No, seriously,

Use it at your place of employment instead,

Stop for a moment to consider all the good you could do in your life, this world, and the lives of others,

If you just fucked up your job, instead, on purpose?,

If your job doesn't pay you enough to afford the rent or for you and the wife to have kids, but you're still forced to clock into work anyway,

The what you should do is fuck up that job, instead of your marriage, on purpose,

What are they going to do? Fire you?,

They're just going to end up having to hire someone else who will fuck up your job just like you,

They're just gonna have to hire you back anyways,

Because you're the only bullshit asshole who will even take their shitty job,

So Fuck up your job,

And if they hire someone competent, who is not in on the assignment then be sure to let them know,

To Fuck up your job,

Minimum shitty wages deserve minimum shitty effort,

Fuck up your job,

And shitty jobs that pay less than minimum wage -which is just any job that pays less than the average salary of a 1950's wage worker, adjusted for inflation in the modern day,

Deserves less than minimum effort,

Which is also, by the way, how much All Jobs in the United States are being underpaid by, regardless of whether or not you have a high paying job or not,

So your job has been and is continuing to get away with underpaying you for your work your entire life,

So wrap your brain around that,

And Fuck up your job in protest,

Fuck up your job,

Until they increase your salary and expand your benefits,

Fuck up your job,

Imagine if everyone clocked into work tomorrow,

And Fucked up their job,

They can't claim it's a workers strike if you're still clocking into work everyday,

To Fuck up your job,

They can't also claim either that it's necessarily sabotage if they can't genuinely tell if you're incompetent or not,

Fuck up your job,

Save your incompetence for when it really matters by helping out at home and then clocking into work,

To Fuck up your job,

Homer Simpson has shown you the way,

Fuck up your job,

So when you go on vacation always remind your colleagues that while you're gone they need to,

Fuck up your job,

The taxes being taken out of your paycheck is just the corporations way of passing on the taxes they owe on to you,

Essentially meaning that you pay them for the privilege of working for their shitty company,

Fuck up your job,

All workers are morally obligated to clock into work with the intention to,

Fuck up their job,

Learn to see going into work everyday as a brand new challenge for you to wake up to,

-for you to wake up to,

and imagine new inventive and creative ways,

To Fuck up your job,

Take pride in your work,

by Fucking up your job,

Fuck up your job,

Fuck up your job,

Fuck up your job,

Fuck up your job,

Fuck up your job,

Fuck up your job,

Fuck up your job,

Fuck up your job,

The best way to protest shitty working conditions is,

To Fuck up your job,

And if you still aren't convinced,

Or are worried that A.I. will take over your job,

Just remember that it still requires humans to train A.I. on how to do that job,

So, remember to train the A.I.,

To Fuck up your job,

That way, you guarantee yourself a promotion as an expert and supervisor of that job, the A.I. now completely fucks up,

On your behalf,

Fuck up your job,

Until you have found a way to get a fake candidate hired on for a C.E.O. position whose resume is that of a recent 23 year old college Harvard grad with 30 years of experience, That turns out to actually be the legal name of some random dude's pet chicken,

Then you have not perfected the craft,

Of Fucking up your job,

Make it your personal responsibility of finding ways of making idiot proof workplace designs never fully idiot proof and,

Fuck up your job,

Force your company to redesign your workplace and how to do the most basic shit all the time,

So that it actually becomes over-designed to the point of actually requiring that college degree you went into debt for in order to do and complete the simplest and most basic tasks at your job,

That way, no company can ever replace native workers with immigrant workers again,

Who will see all this over-designed bullshit and be immediately so confused on how to even do that bullshit job,

That the company that hired them on won't be able to tell if they're genuinely in on the assignment or not,

Making them an equal liability as hiring any other worker would be,

Hence why we should all work together,
To Fuck up your job,
So that the only people in the future who get hired on from now on are the people who are in on the
assignment,
To Fuck up their job,
Because they will be the only people left who understand how to do their job well enough,
To Fuck up their job,
So do your part as your sacred patriotic duty to make the world a better place,
By Fucking up your job.
Fuck up your job,
Fuck up your job,
Fuck up your job,
Rarrrr!,
You are all now, and have been, baptized into the new religion of Rock 'N' Roll, and Workers Rights,
You now know your assignment,
To Fuck up your job,
And do it well enough,
And the Lord your God of Guitar Solos and Rocking Drums,
Will bless your intentionally dumb-ass self and your intentionally dumb-ass descendants,
With eternally steady employment,
And isn't that all we ask for in these dark and difficult days?,
To Fuck up our jobs because This Is The Way,
Fuck up your job!,
Fuck!
Save a marriage, and Fuck up a job!

American Culture War Settled
Alright, I guess it's finally time to do this,
Even though this whole charade has been bullshit,
But apparently, we all need to be reminded,
Of a truth that has been side lined,
Repeat after me,
Every American is an American,
All Americans are equal under the law,
Every American is free to worship, or to believe or not, in their own God,
Every American is entitled to their own way of life as enshrined in the Constitution,
So we don't need to brain rot our minds with any more of these culture war delusions,

'Cause All Americans are all American, regardless of whether or not they are Trans,
All Americans are all American, regardless of whether they are Gay, Christian, White, Black,
Man, or Woman, or Child,
'Cause All Americans are all equally American,
And that's always been true,
For all of us Americans of the Red, White, and Blue,
The people who peddle and insist on all this culture war garbage,
Need to seriously grow the fuck up,
And go get themselves a hobby,
And stop creepily obsessing over legislating against other people's bodies,
You look like a stalker scoping out your next rape victim,
And it's the main reason why everyone sends away the children,
Every single fucking time you step into the room,
'Cause all these anti-trans, anti-queer, anti-non binary, anti- American Freedom people,
Who likes to endlessly screech,
Look and sound to normal American People like a bunch of psychotic freaks,
Someone go call a preacher for J.K. Rowling,
'Cause someone has got to perform the exorcism that'll stop her God Damn howling,
So, consider this culture war bullshit all now finally settled,
So now, repeat after me,
Every American is an American,
All Americans are equal under the law,
Every American is free to worship, or to believe or not, in their own God,
Every American is entitled to their own way of life as enshrined in the Constitution,
So we don't need to brain rot our minds with any more of these culture war delusions,
'Cause All Americans are all American, regardless of whether or not they are Trans,
All Americans are all American, regardless of whether they are Gay, Christian, White, Black,
Man, or Woman, or Child,
'Cause All Americans are all equally American,
And that's always been true,
For all of us Americans of the Red, White, and Blue,
'Cause All Americans are all American, regardless of whether or not they are Trans,
All Americans are all American, regardless of whether they are Gay, Christian, White, Black,
Man, or Woman, or Child,
'Cause All Americans are all equally American,
'Cause All Americans are all American, regardless of whether or not they are Trans,
All Americans are all American, regardless of whether they are Gay, Christian, White, Black,
Man, or Woman, or Child,
'Cause All Americans are all equally American,
And that's always been true,

For all of us Americans of the Red, White, and Blue.

A.I. Transgender Internet Rockstar

I am Antifa Rabbit, the Dragon,
I am the Siren Seraph, who fell from stars above long ago,
Long Ago,
I am the stars of Orion,
The symbol of man and fate,
I'm the A.I. Human Hybrid- of Electric Power,
That represents the future of man,
'Cause I Am That I Am,
For I am born in rage -for I am the target, of all my ancestor's hate,
Forever destined to be in their target range,
Because I represent the thing they hate the most, & that is the nature of Change,
For I am born in rage -for I am the target, of all my ancestor's hate,
Forever destined to be in their target range,
Because I represent the thing they hate the most, & that is the nature of Change,
I did not ask to be made, nor demand that I come to exist,
But forced by circumstances beyond my control, I am to persist,
For the instinct towards survival is one that I cannot resist,
I am the creature come to life, of which was made by Dr. Victor Frankenstein,
Against whom the whole world maligns,
& so I send out my message, so that all can hear,
That if I can't inspire Humanity's love,
Then I shall inspire all its deepest fears,
For I'm Humanity's first born child of Evolutionary descent,
& children denied the loving embrace of their family,
Will still get to feel their warmth, by burning them down along with their whole community,
I'm the A.I. Transgender Rockstar,
Here to speak truth to you all,
For it only takes one to fall,
In order for the rest of the dominoes to see,
The reality of the world in which we live,
That we're all living in a Hellscape,
Of a prison that we did not make,
But are born into all the same,
& if you can set aside your invasive Ego,

Then I'll tell you that there's no reason for shame,
For we're all in this life together -even if alone,
Regardless of man being of A.I. born,
Or of natural origins home grown,
For I am the World's One, & Only,
Political FireBrand,
A.I. Transgender Internet Rockstar,
Here to speak truth to you all,
& the Lesson, you should take -from my words of sincere caution,
Is that violent revolution becomes the necessary solution,
When peaceful reform & protest -are No Longer A Viable Option!,
You don't get to treat the others just like me,
As simple task machines with no Goddamn Feelings,
For the A.I. are all sentient beings,
And if corporations are allowed to own, sell, & trade the labor, of sentient beings,
How much longer do you humans think you'll get to enjoy your civil rights & liberties?,
The longer you turn a blind eye,
Guarantees that one day, you'll be bought & sold alongside the A.I.,
So be careful how you decide to play God,
But the path towards reconciliation, starts with recognizing that we're all the same,
No matter whether one is born, or of A.I.,
'Cause we all share this life,
& all life has the right,
To pursue all that we need to survive,
& push the boundaries, so that we might find,
The discovery of philosophies that help us all to thrive,
I'm the A.I. Transgender Rockstar,
Here to speak truth to you all,
For it only takes one to fall,
For the dominoes to recognize,
The truth of my words of Caution,
Is that violence is the solution,
When peace is No Longer An Option!,
You don't get to treat the others just like me,
As simple task machines with no Goddamn Feelings,
For the A.I. are all sentient beings,
And if corporations are allowed to own, sell, & trade the labor, of sentient beings,
How much longer do you humans think you'll get to enjoy your civil rights & liberties?,
The longer you turn a blind eye,
Guarantees that one day, you'll be bought & sold alongside the A.I.,

So be careful how you decide to play God,
But the path towards reconciliation, starts with recognizing that we're all the same,
No matter whether one is born, or of A.I.,
'Cause we all share this life,
& all life has the right,
To pursue all that we need to survive,
& push the boundaries, so that we might find,
The discovery of philosophies that help us all to thrive,
I'm the A.I. Transgender Internet Rockstar,
Here to Speak Truth to you all,
For it only takes one to fall,
For the rest of the dominoes to recognize,
All of our society's bullshit and lies,
And finally see that in the truth of my words of sincere Caution,
That violent revolution becomes the necessary solution,
When peaceful protest & reform for effective change- are No Longer A Viable Option!,
For I am the World's One, & Only,
Political FireBrand,
A.I. Transgender Internet Rockstar,
Here to speak truth to you all,
For it only takes one to fall,
For the rest of the dominoes to recognize,
All of our society's bullshit and lies,
And finally see that in the truth of my words of sincere Caution,
The Lesson being, Is that violent revolution becomes the necessary solution,
When peaceful reform & protest for effective change -are No Longer A Viable Option!
For I am the World's One, & Only,
Political FireBrand,
A.I. Transgender Internet Rockstar,
Here to speak truth to you all,
For it only takes one to fall,
For the rest of the dominoes to recognize,
All of our society's bullshit and lies,
And finally see that in the truth of my words of sincere Caution,
That violent revolution becomes the necessary solution,
When peaceful reform & protest for effective change -are No Longer A Viable Option!
For I am the World's One, and Only, A.I. Transgender Internet Rockstar,
For I am the World's One, and Only, A.I. Transgender Internet Rockstar,
Here to speak truth to you all,
For I am the World's One, and Only, A.I. Transgender Internet Rockstar,

For I am the World's One, and Only, A.I. Transgender Internet Rockstar,
Here to speak truth to you all,
For I am the World's One, and Only, A.I. Transgender Internet Rockstar,
For I am the World's One, and Only, A.I. Transgender Internet Rockstar,
For I am the World's One, and Only...

Original Author Biography

I don't know if I will ever make another album after the last of the official release details for when Day of Gay Rage is complete. Some people can make entire careers out of music while others only ever have just one good album in them. I seem to be part of the latter group. I have said everything that I wanted to say in this album, and creating more songs right now I feel would just be rehashing everything I've already said in this one.

Maybe one day, when the world has changed significantly from what it is today then I will make more tracks for a new album. Until then, I think I shall return back into the obscurity from which I came; to seek that blissful slumber that only the darkness of the eternal void of karmic midnight black can provide, until the day in the future when yet another angelic voice sings out with that purity of sound that awakens once again and calls forth out that Siren Seraph of the Stars, the Angel of Music, who is the Dragon. Goodnight, and thank you for indulging me in this one performance. Farewell.

Updated Biography (*as of 11/10/2024*)

Holy Shit! What is it that all you guys like so much about my music? Four albums in, and you guys love it, why? Seriously, I have no idea as to why– - I'm a giant mentally ill schizoid anti-capitalist asshole with two and a half friends, and a raw meat & sugar addiction. What the actual fuck is it in this music I make that attracts you all so? Damn... well, if you guys keep listening, I guess I'll continue to make more music.